IMAGES
of America

LINDEN ROW INN

Edgar Allan Poe spent most of his childhood in Richmond, Virginia, and played in a garden owned by Charles Ellis, his adopted father's business partner. That garden plot would eventually become the site of Linden Row. Historians believe that Poe's reference to "an enchanted garden" in one of the many versions of his poem "To Helen" was inspired by his memories of the linden trees, jasmine, and roses that filled his playground. (Courtesy of the Edgar Allan Poe Museum, Richmond, Virginia.)

ON THE COVER: In 1816, Thomas Rutherfoord sold a plot of land to Charles Ellis, who used it as a garden. Ellis, in turn, later sold the land to Fleming James, who built a row of five Greek Revival houses on the eastern end of the block in 1847. The sons of Thomas Rutherfoord purchased the western portion of the block six years later, adding an additional five houses. This rare photograph shows all 10 of the original houses at Linden Row. In 1922, two of the easternmost houses were demolished to make way for a medical office building. Today, seven of the eight remaining homes make up the historic Linden Row Inn, listed in the National Register of Historic Places. (Courtesy of the Valentine Richmond History Center.)

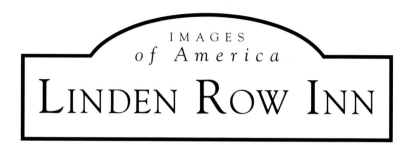

IMAGES
of America

LINDEN ROW INN

Ginger Warder

ARCADIA
PUBLISHING

Published by Arcadia Publishing
Charleston, South Carolina

Printed in the United States of America

Library of Congress Control Number: 2014938390

For all general information, please contact Arcadia Publishing:
Telephone 843-853-2070
Fax 843-853-0044
E-mail sales@arcadiapublishing.com
For customer service and orders:
Toll-Free 1-888-313-2665

Visit us on the Internet at www.arcadiapublishing.com

To my nieces Karen and Jennifer Schroeder and Laura and Sarah Warder, who I'm counting on to preserve our family history for future generations

CONTENTS

ACKNOWLEDGMENTS

This book was a collaborative effort and would not have been possible without the invaluable help of several talented individuals. Joanne McDonald, the archivist at Historic Richmond, and Kelly Kerney, the archivist at the Valentine Richmond History Center, spent hours combing through old photographs to find the lion's share of the historical images in this book, and Casey Watson, the sales manager at Linden Row Inn, spent several more hours scanning them to the correct size.

I am also very grateful to our expert guest writers. David H. Jones, author of the critically acclaimed novel *Two Brothers: One North, One South*, has contributed excellent research and insight into Linden Row's role as a social center of the Confederacy. Chris Semtner, the executive director of the Edgar Allan Poe Museum in Richmond, Virginia, offered commentary on the great writer's connection to the garden at Linden Row and generously shared photographs from his archives.

John Coski at the Museum of the Confederacy shared some of the personal letters of Confederate soldiers from the museum's collection. Richard Lewis at the Virginia Tourism Corporation shared his expertise on Civil War history, as did National Park Service ranger Mike Gorman.

And this book would never have been possible without the support of Vishal Savani and Savara Properties Inc., the current owners of the Linden Row Inn, who value and continue to preserve this historic and architectural landmark. Finally, special thanks to Alfred Scott for sharing his family and personal photographs with us to tell the story of his visionary ancestor, Mary Wingfield Scott, who not only saved Linden Row for posterity, but also helped create the strong preservation community in Richmond that exists today.

INTRODUCTION

Built between 1847 and 1853, the eight remaining Greek Revival row houses that make up the historic Linden Row Inn have played a major role in the history of the capital city of Virginia. And although these architectural treasures, listed in the National Register of Historic Places, are valuable and impressive in their own right, they are also only brick and wood, stone, and decorative ironwork. It is people who make a house a home, and thus, it is the people who have lived and worked at Linden Row since the mid-19th century who are central to its story.

And if houses could talk, these would have many stories to tell: of the wealthy merchants who built the elegant houses; of Edgar Allan Poe playing among the linden trees as a child; of Confederate generals and genteel Southern women gathering here during the War Between the States; of the famous girls' schools and their illustrious pupils; and of an eccentric preservationist who rescued the houses and helped create the Historic Richmond Foundation, which continues to oversee the preservation of Linden Row and many of Richmond's other historic buildings.

In 1785, Thomas Rutherfoord left Scotland and settled in Richmond, becoming one of the city's greatest business leaders of the century. In 1794, he purchased 100 acres west of the city between what are now First and Belvidere Streets, and his brother-in-law William Radford purchased the land between the city and First Street, where Linden Row was built. Near the end of the century, the General Assembly planned to build the state penitentiary on the Radford property, but Rutherfoord opposed the location. He donated 12 acres of land near the river for the prison and purchased the Radford land to preserve it.

In 1816, Rutherfoord sold the eastern end of the Franklin block to Charles Ellis, who used it as a private garden. It was here that Edgar Allan Poe played with the Ellis children: Poe's adopted father, John Allan, was a partner in the Ellis business at the time, and the family lived in a house owned by Ellis on the southwest corner of Second and Franklin Streets. In later years, Poe courted his first love, Elmira Royster, in that same garden.

In 1839, Ellis sold the garden land to Fleming James, who, five years later, built a row of five houses on the eastern end of the block, known as Linden Square. In 1853, the sons of Thomas Rutherfoord bought the western portion of the block and built an additional five houses. At least some of the homes were designed by Richmond-born architect Otis Manson and are still revered today as among the city's finest examples of the Greek Revival style.

During the Civil War, Linden Row was a social gathering place for the leaders of the Confederacy, as well as home to two prestigious schools for girls. D. Lee Powell and his wife purchased the houses at 100 and 102 East Franklin Street in 1853 and operated a boarding school, the Southern Female Institute. In 1863, one of Powell's students, Elizabeth Maxwell Alsop, wrote in her journal, "General Jackson was wounded in the battle of Chancellorsville and after seeming to improve for several days, suddenly began to sink and died half past three, Sunday evening, May 10. That was a dearly bought victory. Tuesday evening, Mr. Powell took us all down to take a last, long look at the people's idol. I regret so much not having taken a flower from his coffin to keep in remembrance of that day."

Also living at Linden Row during these years was the Pegram family. James West Pegram was a general in the Virginia Militia and the president of the Bank of Virginia. After his death in a steamboat explosion, his wife, Virginia Johnson Pegram, moved her five children to 106 and 108 East Franklin Street and, with her daughter, Mary, opened a school.

Virginia Pegram's three sons all served in the Confederate army, and Linden Row was a center of social activity for them and their friends. James West Pegram Jr. served on the staffs of Generals Richard Ewell and Lewis A. Armistead. William became known as one of Robert E. Lee's hardest-fighting artillerymen. John Pegram, the oldest son, was a brigadier general in Lee's army. John married Hetty Cary, known as one of the most beautiful belles of the South. Their wedding, held at St. Paul's Episcopal Church on January 19, 1865, was reported to be the social event of the season. Sadly, three weeks to the day after the wedding, General Pegram's funeral was held in the same church after he was killed in battle.

In 1895, Virginia Randolph Ellet moved her girls' school to 112 East Franklin Street in Linden Row; eventually, that school became what is known today as St. Catherine's. Many prominent Richmond ladies, including the Langhorne sisters, were educated at Virginia Ellet's school for girls, locally known as "Miss Jennie's School." Nancy Langhorne became Lady Astor, the first woman to serve in the British House of Commons, while her sister Irene became known as the "Gibson Girl."

In the late 19th and early 20th centuries, Linden Row continued to be a prominent address in Richmond, housing *Lewis Rand* author Mary Johnston, along with well-known families, including the Montagues. Helen Lefroy Caperton grew up at Linden Row during those years and reminisced about her childhood in a 1949 article in the *Richmond Times*: "Our usual breakfast consisted of hot rolls, beaten biscuits, batter bread, batter cakes or waffles, chicken or turkey hash, eggs as you wanted them, ham carved in chiffon pink slices, and always, without fail, a dish of fat roe herrings. Had any of us said 'I take only fruit juice and coffee, please' he would have been regarded as mildly insane, and Mary Jefferson, who for 53 years cooked for my grandparents, would have been wounded to the quick."

Helen Caperton's grandparents, Mr. and Mrs. John H. Montague, lived at 118 East Franklin Street, one of the two houses torn down in 1922 to make way for the Medical Arts building. By the middle of the century, the houses of Linden Row had been converted into apartments and shops, and Franklin Street was becoming a business district rather than a residential area. Local preservationist Mary Wingfield Scott, who had attended Miss Jennie's School at Linden Row, led the movement to found the William Byrd Branch of the Association for the Preservation of Virginia Antiquities in 1935 to save the Adam Craig House. She was highly respected as an architectural historian. The wealthy and eccentric Scott purchased seven of the remaining eight homes at Linden Row in the 1950s, operating them as apartments. In 1980, she donated them to the Historic Richmond Foundation. The foundation in turn sold the property and supervised the renovations and conversion of Linden Row into the Linden Row Inn and retains a supervisory interest in the property in perpetuity. Savara Properties Inc. has owned and operated Linden Row Inn since 2008 and is committed to preserving this historic gem for future generations.

One

EDGAR ALLAN POE'S ENCHANTED GARDEN AT LINDEN ROW

Readers around the globe know author Edgar Allan Poe (1809–1849) as a master of the macabre and the inventor of the detective story, but few realize he also loved gardens. Throughout his brief life, Poe praised the beauty of gardens in poetry, short stories, and essays. In "The Domain of Arnheim," the author theorized that the landscape garden was an art form superior to painting, sculpture, even poetry. In one version of his poem "To Helen," Poe referred to an "enchanted garden." The garden that may have inspired this reference and Poe's lifelong love of gardening once stood on the site now occupied by the Linden Row Inn.

When he was 11, Poe moved with his foster parents, John and Frances Valentine Allan, into the large frame house that once stood across the street to the southwest corner of Second and Franklin Streets. The owner of both this home and the garden was John Allan's business partner Charles Ellis.

While living in the Ellis house, the future author was a master prankster known to pull chairs out from under ladies at dinner and chase Ellis's daughter with a toy snake. Ellis's son Thomas Ellis recalled in the May 7, 1881, issue of the *Richmond Standard* that Poe was "a leader among boys" who led him "to do many things for which [he] was punished." Poe also taught Thomas "to shoot, to swim and to skate, [and] to play bandy" and even once saved him from drowning in the James River.

After moving out of the neighborhood, Poe would return frequently to the Ellis garden. By this time, the walled garden contained so many roses that Richmond historian Samuel Mordecai recalled in *Richmond in By-Gone Days* that one could smell the blooms from a block away. The garden had become a popular meeting spot for young lovers, and the 16-year-old poet courted his first fiancée, Elmira Royster, there. Although her father disapproved of the match, Poe and Royster became secretly engaged. Unfortunately, Royster's father intercepted Poe's letters to her from college, convincing her that Poe had forgotten about her. By the time Poe returned from his first (and last) term at the University of Virginia, Royster had engaged herself to another man. In a few months, Poe would run away from home to begin his life as a poet, publishing his first book at the age of 18.

Chris Semtner, executive director
The Edgar Allan Poe Museum, Richmond, Virginia

Edgar Poe was born in Boston in 1809, but he always called Richmond home and referred to himself as a Virginian. His mother, Elizabeth Poe (pictured), an actress with a traveling company, was performing at the Richmond Theatre in 1811 when she fell ill and died, leaving her two young children, two-year-old Edgar and his infant sister, Rosalie. Both children were adopted by Richmond families: Edgar was taken in by John and Frances Valentine Allan, and Rosalie by William and Jane Scott MacKenzie. John Allan, a partner in the Ellis and Allan mercantile firm, gave Poe his middle name. At that time, the family lived above the firm's office at Thirteenth and East Main Streets, later moving to a house owned by Charles Ellis on Franklin Street. (Courtesy of the Edgar Allan Poe Museum, Richmond.)

Poe's mother, Elizabeth, was buried in the churchyard of St. John's Episcopal Church, where her memorial stone still stands. The first church built in Richmond and completed in 1741, St. John's is known for its role in the Revolutionary War. In 1775, more than 100 of Virginia's leaders, including Patrick Henry, Thomas Jefferson, George Washington, Richard Henry Lee, and Peyton Randolph, met here for the Second Virginia Convention. On March 23, 1775, Patrick Henry delivered his rousing "Give me liberty or give me death" speech, which helped the resolutions pass by a narrow margin. The American Revolution began a month later, when shots were fired at Concord and Lexington. Many figures in Richmond and Virginia history are buried here, in what was Richmond's first public cemetery, including George Wythe and Chief Justice John Marshall. St. John's Church was designated a National Historic Landmark in 1961. (Courtesy of the Valentine Richmond History Center.)

The Allans and their adopted son Edgar lived for a time in a house owned by Charles Ellis, John Allan's business partner. Ellis also owned the land diagonally across the street, which he used as a private garden. The Allans took Poe to England for about five years but returned to Richmond, where he spent his childhood years. (Courtesy of the Edgar Allan Poe Museum, Richmond.)

Frances Valentine Allan's room in the Ellis house shows typical architectural details of Richmond's early-19th-century homes, including pocket doors and fireplaces. The Poe Museum in Richmond owns a number of pieces of furniture from the Allan homes, including Edgar Allan Poe's boyhood bed. (Courtesy of the Edgar Allan Poe Museum, Richmond.)

Historians believe this oil-on-tin portrait of John Allan was most likely painted by popular artist Thomas Sully around 1804. Sully's ledger lists several portraits of friends of the Allans, and Sully was living in Richmond at that time. The portrait is part of the collection at the Poe Museum in Richmond. (Courtesy of the Edgar Allan Poe Museum, Richmond.)

Sully's companion portrait to John Allan's, that of his wife, Frances, was lost, but his nephew, Robert Sully, painted this copy, which hangs in the Poe Museum among the collection of items from the Allan family. Frances, often called Franny, was a member of Richmond's prestigious Valentine family. (Courtesy of the Edgar Allan Poe Museum, Richmond.)

Edgar Allan Poe's childhood hero was Lord Byron. Even as a child, Poe (pictured) always wanted to be a writer. In fact, some of his early verses were found on the back of his adopted father's ledger sheets. He courted Elmira Royster among the roses and linden trees of the Ellis garden, and they became engaged before he left for the University of Virginia in 1826. (Courtesy of the Edgar Allan Poe Museum, Richmond.)

John Allan was a miser and sent Poe to college with less than half of the money he needed. When Poe began running up gambling debts while attending the University of Virginia, his relationship with Allan deteriorated. By the end of the term, Poe was forced to burn his furniture to keep warm. Furious with Allan, Poe returned to Richmond to find that his fiancée, Elmira Royster (pictured here), had become engaged to another man. (Courtesy of the Edgar Allan Poe Museum, Richmond.)

Linden Row was originally called Linden Square, and both names derive from the many linden trees on the property. When Edgar Allan Poe played here as a child, in addition to the linden trees, the garden was filled with roses and jasmine. A portion of the original garden remains in the courtyard behind the Linden Row Inn, a popular venue for weddings. (Courtesy of the Edgar Allan Poe Museum, Richmond.)

After the death of her husband, Alexander Barrett Shelton, Poe's first fiancée, Elmira Royster Shelton, rented this home on Church Hill across from St. John's Church. When Poe returned to Richmond in 1849, he visited her often, and they eventually became engaged for the second time. (Courtesy of the Edgar Allan Poe Museum, Richmond.)

Elmira Royster's father, James Royster, disapproved of Edgar Allan Poe and intercepted the letters Poe wrote to Elmira from college. James Royster convinced his daughter that Poe had forgotten her, and he encouraged her to break the engagement and marry Alexander Shelton, a wealthy businessman. This miniature of James Royster was donated to the Poe Museum by Elmira Shelton's descendants. (Courtesy of the Edgar Allan Poe Museum, Richmond.)

Edgar Allan Poe's only sister, Rosalie, was less than a year old when their mother, Elizabeth, died. Rosalie was taken in by William and Jane Scott Mackenzie and attended the prestigious Mackenzie's School for Girls, run by her foster mother's sister-in-law. She later taught penmanship at that same school. (Courtesy of the Edgar Allan Poe Museum, Richmond.)

In 1847, Poe's wife, Virginia Clemm, died, and in 1849, he returned to Richmond and became engaged for the second time to Elmira Royster Shelton. On September 27, he left Richmond for New York. Days later, the author was found delirious in Baltimore. He died on October 7, 1849. (Courtesy of the Edgar Allan Poe Museum, Richmond.)

One of the oldest remaining houses in Richmond, the Old Stone House, has been home to the Edgar Allan Poe Museum since 1922. The *Southern Literary Messenger*, where Poe first worked in Richmond, was also located on Main Street, west of the Old Stone House. The museum houses one of the world's finest collections of manuscripts, letters, photographs, first editions, and personal belongings of this American literary genius. (Courtesy of the Valentine Richmond History Center.)

Two

Linden Row during the Civil War and Reconstruction

Richmond brims with monumental sites that memorialize great events. Less obvious among its structures are places that witnessed the wide range of human triumphs and tragedies experienced by wartime residents. Visiting these special places and quietly reflecting upon the significance of what occurred there can evoke a welling of emotion that creates a bond with previous generations.

Such a spot is Mrs. Pegram's Parlor, an important room in the Linden Row residence of Virginia Pegram that also served as a school for young ladies. Given the social and military prominence of the Pegram family, the parlor witnessed many events involving the most distinguished inhabitants of the capital city. At one time or another, many of them were there to celebrate jubilant moments or to commiserate over catastrophes suffered during those tumultuous years.

The happy events were often celebrations of military promotions and battlefield exploits of the three Pegram sons, James, John, and William. Other good times revolved around teas and parties when great and celebrated persons visited Mrs. Pegram and her daughter Mary, who was known for her striking and stimulating personality. Hetty Cary unexpectedly returned from one of her secret forays in support of the Confederate cause and arrived at a party in Mrs. Pegram's Parlor adorned in a beautiful Baltimore ball gown to the surprise and delight of all, especially her future husband, Gen. John Pegram.

Their wedding at St Paul's in January 1865 was the highlight of a dreadful winter season. However, that celebration turned to profound sorrow when John's casket rested in the same chancel, three weeks to the day after his marriage to the beautiful Cary. The declining fortunes of war brought more sadness to the Pegram home when it was learned that Col. Willie Pegram had died defending his guns at Five Forks.

If a visitor focuses upon the enormity of what these people endured, the walls of Mrs. Pegram's Parlor, preserved as Parlour Suite 220 in the historic Linden Row Inn, will tell stories about the luminaries of the Confederacy who shared both joy and grief in this special place.

David H. Jones, author
Two Brothers: One North, One South

After Virginia Johnson Pegram lost her husband in a steamboat explosion, she moved her children to 106–108 East Franklin Street, where she created a school for young ladies to support her family. Her daughter, Mary, helped with the school and looked after her younger sister, Virginia, while her three sons, John (pictured), James West, and William, left Richmond to fight for the Confederacy. The Pegram home was a gathering place for Richmond society and for leaders of the Confederate army and government. Mary, known for her vivacious personality, was a consummate hostess. In fact, Brig. Gen. John Pegram, her son, met his future bride, Hetty Cary, at a social soirée in the Pegram parlor. From their home in Linden Row, Virginia and Mary could watch Confederate soldiers marching down Franklin Street or occasionally hear the canon fire of nearby battles. Sadly, only one of Pegram's sons survived the war to return to Richmond. (Courtesy of the Valentine Richmond History Center.)

Prominent socialite Hetty Cary (pictured here) met John Pegram at a party at the Pegram residence at Linden Row, and they were married just three weeks before he was killed. (Courtesy of www.richmondthenandnow.com)

The Museum of the Confederacy in Richmond has an extensive archive of letters from Confederate soldiers. In a letter dated December 22, 1864, Col. William Pegram wrote to his mother in Richmond, confessing to late evenings of partying near Petersburg. "By the time I reached camp and got to bed, it was quarter to four, and the next night (Tuesday) I went to a party at Col. Walker's and got to bed at a quarter to five," he wrote. In the same letter, he wrote of his homesickness and of his older brother's romance with the beautiful Hetty Cary, saying, "I wish very much that I could be there with you all now." Of John Pegram and Hetty Cary, William wrote, "How I wish that they could be married." (Both, courtesy of the Museum of the Confederacy.)

Sgt. Tucker Randolph, a young Richmond officer who served on Gen. John Pegram's staff, also wrote home frequently from the various camps as the army was on the move. On November 12, 1862, Randolph wrote, "As you see, I am still in Knoxville killing time, we are waiting for Kirby Smith to give us orders and there is also rather bad news for me. Genl. John Pegram is to be assigned to Col Ashby Brigade which throws him back to his Regt and me back to the Company, which I am very sorry for, as my position in it is very disagreeable. Is there an opening that you know of in or about Richmond, I believe I had rather fight in the Old Dominion than any place else." In a letter dated May 23, 1864, Randolph wrote from the headquarters of Pegram's Brigade near Hanover Junction, detailing troop movements and battle details, but noting, "Genl Lee is in glorious spirits we saw him yesterday, so we think all is going on right. Such is the advantage in having confidence in the commander of the Army." Sadly, just a week later, in a letter dated May 31, the Randolphs were notified of Tucker's death. (Both, courtesy of the Museum of the Confederacy.)

Richmond City Hall, pictured here in 1865, was a modest structure located at Eleventh and Capitol Streets. It was rebuilt 20 years later in the popular postwar Victorian Gothic style and became one of the most iconic buildings in Richmond. (Courtesy of the Valentine Richmond History Center.)

Main Street, one block south of Franklin Street, has always been a center of commerce and banking in Richmond. Both Main Street and Cary Street, one block south, suffered major damage at the end of the Civil War; many of the antebellum homes and commercial buildings ended up in ruins. (Courtesy of the Valentine Richmond History Center.)

The owner of the Haxall Flour Mills, Bolling Haxall, was a staunch Confederate supporter. He constructed what some historians believe was an escape tunnel on the lower level of the house at 211 East Franklin Street (pictured). In 1860, Richmond was the nation's leader in flour milling, and many prosperous merchants, like Haxall, lived on Franklin Street. However, the Evacuation Fire destroyed the Haxall Mills, and Bolling Haxall fled the city on April 2, 1865. The mills were partially rebuilt after the war, but they never fully rebounded, and Haxall sold the house in 1869. (Courtesy of Historic Richmond.)

Designed by noted Boston architect Alexander Parris, the Neoclassical governor's mansion is the oldest inhabited governor's mansion in the United States. Located on Capitol Square, the mansion survived the Evacuation Fire in 1865 and another fire in 1926 started by a Christmas tree. An oval dining room was added on the back in 1906, and restorations on both the interior and exterior took place in the 20th century. The brick kitchen and stables, two of the original outbuildings, have also been restored. (Courtesy of the Valentine Richmond History Center.)

Located at 707 East Franklin Street, this Greek Revival house was one of five row homes built by wealthy tobacco merchant Norman Stewart between 1844 and 1849. When Stewart died in 1856, he left the building to his nephew, who rented it to Gen. George Washington Custis Lee, Robert E. Lee's son, for use as a "bachelor's mess" for Confederate officers. The Stewart-Lee House is more widely known as the Robert E. Lee House, since the Confederate general and his family lived here after the confiscation of their home in Arlington in 1864. The only surviving house of the original row, it was once used as the headquarters for the Historic Richmond Foundation. Today, it houses office space. (Both, courtesy of the Valentine Richmond History Center.)

Built by Chief Justice John Marshall in the late 1700s, this brick Federal-style house was Marshall's home for 45 years and belonged to his family until 1911. When it was slated for demolition, the public protested vehemently, and it was purchased by Preservation Virginia in 1913. Today, it is open to the public for tours. (Courtesy of the Valentine Richmond History Center.)

St. John's Church has not changed much over the past three centuries, and it looks much the same today as it did during the Civil War and the Revolutionary War. It was at St. John's that Patrick Henry gave his incendiary speech, "Give me liberty or give me death." Many notable figures in American history, including George Wythe, one of the signers of the Declaration of Independence, are buried at St. John's. The church, built around 1741, is located in Church Hill, Richmond's oldest neighborhood, which sits on a hill overlooking the city. (Courtesy of the Valentine Richmond History Center.)

Built in 1844, St. Paul's Episcopal Church was attended by most of the leaders of the Confederacy, including Jefferson Davis and Robert E. Lee. Gen. John Pegram (left) met the beautiful Hetty Cary of Baltimore at one of the many parties at Linden Row that his sister, Mary, hosted throughout the war. They were married at St. Paul's in what was certainly one of the biggest social events of the season. Sadly, three weeks to the day after John and Hetty's wedding, the same guests returned to St. Paul's for John Pegram's funeral. He had been killed at Hatcher's Run, west of Petersburg. (Both, courtesy of the Valentine Richmond History Center.)

During the war, Tredegar Iron Works produced the majority of cannons used by the Confederacy. On nearby Brown's Island, the Confederate States Laboratory manufactured ammunition until March 13, 1863, when the laboratory was destroyed in an explosion. The *Richmond Examiner* reported, "Similar sounding explosions, arising from the trial of ordnance at the Tredegar Iron Works, had been daily heard in that neighborhood, and it was some minutes before a dense smoke arising from the island apprised the citizens of the true cause of the explosion." (Courtesy of the Valentine Richmond History Center.)

Reflecting the broad range of architectural styles that flourished in Richmond in the 19th century, Monumental Church was designed by Robert Mills, America's first native-born professional architect. The Neoclassical design, an octagonal shape capped with a dome, was probably inspired by Thomas Jefferson, as Mills was a student of Jefferson's signature style. Built between 1812 and 1814, the church sits on the site of the former Richmond Theatre, destroyed by a fire on December 26, 1811. The fire claimed the lives of more than 72 people, including the governor. Under the front portico of the church, a monument is inscribed with the names of those who perished. (Courtesy of Historic Richmond.)

In 1780, Virginia's state capital moved from Williamsburg to Richmond. Shockoe Hill was chosen as the site for the new government building. Designed by Thomas Jefferson, the Neoclassical capitol is the first full-scale building in the form of a Classical temple built since antiquity. Jefferson consulted with Charles-Louis Clerisseau on the design, and Clerisseau created a plaster model of the building. The front steps and wings were added in 1906, and another addition was completed in 2007, but the building looks much today as it did in 1788 when it was first occupied. In 1818, the cast-iron fence was added; it is one of the oldest and largest surviving fences of its kind in the country. In 1850, John Notman redesigned the grounds, adding fountains and wide, curving paths. This photograph shows the rubble of the destruction of the city during the final days of the Civil War. (Courtesy of the Valentine Richmond History Center.)

Renowned Civil War photographer Mathew Brady took this photograph of the Tredegar Iron Works in 1865. Prior to the Civil War, this industrial complex produced the elaborate iron railings, decorative fencing, and gates that graced the finest homes in Richmond. Many of the homes on Franklin Street, including those at Linden Row, still retain their original ironwork details. Tredegar was vital to the Confederate war effort, producing the largest number of cannons used by the South. Today, the Richmond Civil War Visitors Center is located in one of the surviving buildings, and free tours of the grounds are conducted by National Park Service rangers. (Courtesy of the Valentine Richmond History Center/National Archives.)

Tredegar Iron Works suffered major damage in the fall of Richmond, and the nearby railroad trestle was completely destroyed. Confederate president Jefferson Davis managed to flee Richmond by train on these same tracks across the James River, just before Richmond fell to Union forces. In the photograph to the left, visible behind the ruined train tracks, is Belle Isle, where noncommissioned Union officers and privates were held as prisoners of war. Although there was a hospital for the prisoners, there were no barracks, and the captured Union troops were forced to stay in tents, in both extreme cold and extreme heat. Today, Belle Isle is a favorite park for hiking, jogging, and picnics. It is connected to the mainland by a footbridge. Tredegar Iron Works is an official National Park Service Visitor Center and also home to the American Civil War Center. (Both, courtesy of the Valentine Richmond History Center.)

In this Mathew Brady photograph, Yankees stand on the back veranda of the Jefferson Davis house, heralding the end of the conflict. The White House of the Confederacy, home to Pres. Jefferson Davis and his family during the war, still contains more than half of its original furnishings. Guided tours of the former executive mansion are offered daily, in combination with the nearby Museum of the Confederacy. The mansion has been meticulously restored, enabling visitors to see it as it looked when it was the political center of the Confederacy. Unfortunately, 20th-century development of the Virginia Commonwealth University Hospital has surrounded the home and blocked what was once a commanding view of the city. (Courtesy of the Valentine Richmond History Center.)

Steven Spielberg's 2012 movie *Lincoln*, starring Daniel Day-Lewis as Pres. Abraham Lincoln and Sally Field as Mary Todd Lincoln, was filmed on location in Richmond and Petersburg. Spielberg filmed several scenes at the state capitol. This photograph of the capitol building, taken three days after the fall of Richmond, shows the building as it was when Lincoln visited in the last months of his life in 1865, when he was lobbying to pass the 13th Amendment, as detailed in Spielberg's historical drama. Today, the main building of the capitol, designed by Thomas Jefferson, looks much the same, although wings have been added on either side over the years. (Courtesy of the Valentine Richmond History Center.)

Robert Pegram, born in 1869, was the son of James West Pegram, the only surviving son of Virginia Pegram. Robert was a celebrated naval officer who served in the Mexican War, in Paraguay, and in Japan and was awarded a special sword by the Virginia General Assembly for his service. His father, James Pegram, and his grandfather, Gen. John Pegram, were also highly regarded military men. (Courtesy of the Valentine Richmond History Center.)

One branch of the Pegram family lived in Dinwiddie County, near Petersburg. Mary Louise Pegram, born on October 3, 1865, is buried in Petersburg's Blandford Cemetery, along with many other members of this branch of the family. Blandford Cemetery is known as one of the earliest sites of Memorial Day celebrations, a tradition started by Virginia's leading ladies to pay tribute to fallen Confederate soldiers. Women, considered nonpolitical, led the campaigns through their Ladies Memorial Associations to raise funds for national and regional Confederate cemeteries, a task that may have been considered treasonous if former Confederate soldiers had attempted it. (Courtesy of the Valentine Richmond History Center.)

Robert Pegram's sisters, Lucy Cargill Pegram (pictured left) and Emma "Emcie" Blacknall Pegram (pictured with Lucy below), were also born after the Civil War. Their parents are buried in Richmond's Hollywood Cemetery. (Both, courtesy of the Valentine Richmond History Center.)

Broad Street in the 1870s was lined with popular restaurants and shops, just as it is today. A horse and buggy stands in front of John Murphy's Restaurant at 810 East Broad Street. Mary Wingfield Scott extensively researched early Richmond for her book *Houses of Old Richmond* and describes the city during this era: "From 1810 to 1867 Richmond was bounded, roughly, by the James River on the south, by a line parallel to Belvidere Street, but about two blocks east of it on the west; by Federal Street running northeast to where the Seaboard tracks now are, and then following Broad Street on east from Eighteenth to Thirteenth Streets, the line then turning to Nicholson Street and thence to the river. These boundaries are important to visualize if we would understand how many old homes now in the heart of town were suburban farmhouses when they were built." (Courtesy of the Valentine Richmond History Center.)

In the 1870s, horses and covered wagons were still prominently used for trade. Broad Street was, as it is today, the main street for commerce in the city. This photograph shows the north side of Broad and Sixth Streets. (Courtesy of the Valentine Richmond History Center.)

In this photograph of the northeast corner of Second and Franklin Streets, Linden Row is not visible. It is a block farther west on Franklin Street. These buildings have been replaced with a fire station and parking garage. (Courtesy of the Valentine Richmond History Center.)

The Commercial Café at 912 East Main Street was most likely frequented by the many merchants on Main and Broad Streets. The window advertises oysters, and the display of fowl suggests a true farm-to-table cuisine. Today, many downtown Richmond restaurants still feature oysters from the nearby Chesapeake Bay, and while they do not display their proteins, many of the city's best chefs source their ingredients regionally. (Courtesy of the Valentine Richmond History Center.)

The James River, which runs through the center of Richmond, returned to a peaceful, recreational state after the war. Although Abraham Lincoln's efforts to create and pass the 13th Amendment ended slavery, many Southerners continued to believe strongly in the tenets of what was labeled "The Lost Cause": that the secession was more about states' rights than slavery, and that slavery was a benign institution. In fact, although African Americans were free citizens after the war, many continued to work as domestic servants for well-to-do Southerners. (Courtesy of the Valentine Richmond History Center.)

From 1853 to 1865, the D. Lee Powell Southern Female Institute occupied 100 and 102 East Franklin Street (the westernmost houses) at Linden Row. In 1862, as the battle of the Peninsula campaign raged east of Richmond, Lee Powell escorted his boarding students out of the city to a safer location. One of them, Elizabeth Maxwell Alsop of Fredericksburg, wrote in her journal on June 29, "Hurrah for the Southern Confederacy!!! Joy! Joy! Joy! Glorious news. Telegraphic dispatches revealed McClellan's Army in retreat our army pursuing. Already they have gotten so far that the guns cannot be heard in Richmond." By October, the boarding students had returned to Powell's school at Linden Row. The two homes on the far right of this photograph, at 116 and 118 East Franklin Street, on the east end of the row, were torn down in 1922. (Courtesy of Alfred Scott.)

After Reconstruction, Southern social events resumed at full swing in Richmond. Every season showcased a formal ball. Here, Mrs. Thomas Bolling is decked out in a period costume for the Colonial Ball in 1890. Ladies creatively renovated their prewar gowns. (Courtesy of the Valentine Richmond History Center.)

Formal cotillions were known as "germans," referring to the name of a dance called the German. Gentlemen, such as Thomas Bolling, wore their Prince Alberts, flared frock coats with a tightly cinched waist that had been stored away during the war. Bolling is an old Virginia family name. In fact, Thomas Jefferson's older sister Mary married a Bolling. (Courtesy of the Valentine Richmond History Center.)

The White House of the Confederacy was abandoned during the evacuation of Richmond on April 2, 1865. Later, during Reconstruction, it was used as the headquarters for Military District No. 1 of Virginia and as the residence of some of the commanding officers of the Department of Virginia. In 1870, after Reconstruction ended, the City of Richmond resumed possession of the house and later used it as one of the first public schools in the city, Richmond Central School. In 1890, the city planned to demolish the White House to build a modern school, but the Confederate Memorial Literary Society was formed with the express purpose of saving the house. (Both, courtesy of the Valentine Richmond History Center.)

Three

20TH-CENTURY RICHMOND AND LINDEN ROW'S FAMOUS RESIDENTS

Fortunately, Linden Row and the neighboring mansions on Franklin Street were not damaged during the fall of Richmond or in the Evacuation Fire of 1865 at the end of the war. In the early 1900s, Linden Row continued to be both a prestigious address and the home to another popular school for girls, operated by Virginia Randolph Ellett at 112 East Franklin Street. Virginia Ellett's school for girls, locally known as Miss Jennie's School, moved in 1917 to a location in Westhampton. In 1920, it was incorporated into the diocesan schools of the Episcopal Church and renamed St. Catherine's. It is still operating today.

Miss Jennie's School was attended by many prominent Virginia women, including Mary Wingfield Scott, the architectural historian and preservationist who saved Linden Row from destruction later in the century. Other famous pupils included Nancy and Irene Langhorne. Nancy eventually became Lady Astor, the first woman to be elected to Britain's House of Commons. Irene married artist Charles Dana Gibson and inspired his drawings of beautiful Southern women that became known as the "Gibson Girl."

Author Mary Johnston called 110 East Franklin Street home for six years. While living at Linden Row, she published one of her most well-known novels, *Lewis Rand*, the story of a young politician in early Richmond. One of Richmond's most prominent families, that of Mr. and Mrs. John H. Montague, also lived at Linden Row at 118 East Franklin Street, one of the two houses torn down in 1922 to make way for the Medical Arts building. John Montague was the first president of the Richmond German, an elaborate cotillion with strict etiquette and an even stricter, white-glove dress code. His granddaughter Helena Lefroy Caperton was born and raised at Linden Row and fondly recalls the genteel lifestyle and social events of the day, including the annual New Year's Day open houses. "These functions began at noon on New Year's Day and continued indefinitely. If for any reason you were not entertaining, you hung an elaborate gilded basket with a ribbon bow onto the front door, in which everyone left cards," she noted in a letter to the *Richmond Times* in 1949.

Unfortunately, the destruction of 116 and 118 East Franklin Street in 1922 heralded the beginning of the commercialization of Franklin Street and the end of an era of gracious, residential living.

Located at 101 West Franklin Street, the Jefferson Hotel is one of a handful of prestigious hotels in America to hold both the five-star and five-diamond designation. This Beaux-Arts beauty was built in 1895 and designed by New York architects Carrére and Hastings, who also designed the main branch of the New York Public Library. It was the brainchild of Maj. Lewis Ginter, one of Richmond's wealthiest businessmen and biggest philanthropists. The Palm Court lobby retains its original Tiffany windows and a life-sized statue of Thomas Jefferson created by Richmond sculptor Edward Valentine. A fire in 1901 partially destroyed the hotel, but the statue was rescued, and the hotel was rebuilt with the addition of a grand staircase leading from the mezzanine level to the lower (original) lobby. The hotel sits on the site of the former home of Mary Pegram and her husband, Gen. James Anderson. (Photograph by Richard Creek, courtesy of Historic Richmond.)

The Bowers Brothers building was located in Shockoe Slip. Richmond exported its fine flour and Virginia tobacco, and returning ships brought coffee, tea, and spices, which Bower Brothers sold. Since goods were delivered by horse-drawn wagons and many customers arrived on horseback or in a horse-drawn carriage, the merchants provided a water fountain for horses. (Courtesy of Historic Richmond.)

In the above panoramic photograph, Richmond is seen in the early 1900s. The damage to the city from the war and the Evacuation Fire of 1865 had become a distant memory. Once again, the state capital bustled as a center of trade. The photograph below shows Broad Street above First Street, just a few blocks from Linden Row. As seen here, a trolley line coexists with horse-and-buggy traffic. (Both, courtesy of the Valentine Richmond History Center.)

The above photograph, taken in 1905, shows the 700 block of East Franklin Street, looking west behind the First Market. Horse-drawn covered wagons, reminiscent of the pioneers, were used to transport goods to and from the market. Below, an ice wagon travels down East Broad Street in the early 1900s, past shops, restaurants, and hotels. (Both, courtesy of the Valentine Richmond History Center.)

Helena Lefroy Caperton grew up at Linden Row, at 118 East Franklin Street (far right), the home of her grandparents, Mr. and Mrs. John H. Montague. On April 17, 1949 in the *Richmond Times*, she wrote, "Then, Linden Row really deserved its name, for in each front yard, there grew a majestic linden tree, reaching as high as the third story windows. They were dramatic in their leafing, for as I remember those springtimes, it used to seem that overnight the tree would burst out into a wealth of bright green foliage; a green more sharply exquisite than that of any other tree, being an almost perfect chartreuse." By the time this photograph was taken in 1915, the transition of Franklin Street from a residential neighborhood to a business district was well under way. The Montague home, as well as its neighbor, 116 East Franklin Street, were torn down in 1922 to make way for the Medical Arts building. (Courtesy of the Valentine Richmond History Center.)

Built in 1845 in the Colonial Revival style, the Kent-Valentine House at 12 East Franklin Street is hard to recognize today, as a Classical portico replaced the original iron veranda. However, the original carriage house remains. The entire house was restored in the 1970s. Today, it is the headquarters for the Garden Club of Virginia. (Courtesy of the Valentine Richmond History Center.)

This early-20th-century photograph of Linden Row shows all 10 of the original homes. Once called Richmond's Fifth Avenue, Franklin Street in the 18th and 19th centuries was home to the city's most prosperous citizens, many of them merchants. The neighborhood west of the capitol and south of Broad Street, known as Monroe Ward, was once one of the most coveted addresses in the city. It features a wide variety of architectural styles, including Greek Revival, Queen Anne, Italianate, and Beaux-Arts. Fortunately, these beautiful homes were largely untouched by the destruction of Richmond and the evacuation fire at the end of the Civil War. Today, most of the remaining mansions have been converted into office space or apartments or, in the case of Linden Row, into a historic inn. (Courtesy of the Valentine Richmond History Center.)

Located at 211 East Franklin Street, just west of the Linden Row Inn, the Bolling Haxall mansion was sold in 1869. Since 1900, it has been occupied by the Woman's Club and is a popular venue for weddings. The antebellum house features cast-iron fencing, window arches, and balconies made in Richmond before the war. The interior boasts a stunning spiral staircase (below) and ornate woodwork and is furnished with period antiques. (Both, courtesy of the Valentine Richmond History Center.)

Built in the same time period as Linden Row, between 1854 and 1857, the Leigh Street Baptist Church is a fine example of the Greek Revival architecture popular in the mid-19th century. It features a Grecian Doric pedimental portico with six fluted columns. Located in historic Church Hill, the building was used as a hospital for Confederate soldiers during the Civil War. Listed in the National Register of Historic Places, Leigh Street Baptist Church is the oldest Baptist church in the city to continuously occupy the same space, and it is still an active ministry today. In 1930, the church was enlarged and the interior was entirely refurbished. (Both, courtesy of the Valentine Richmond History Center.)

Students, like these from Chimborazo School in 1907, often wore simple uniforms. Many schools, like Virginia Ellet's school for girls at Linden Row, were privately owned or were operated by churches. (Courtesy of Historic Richmond.)

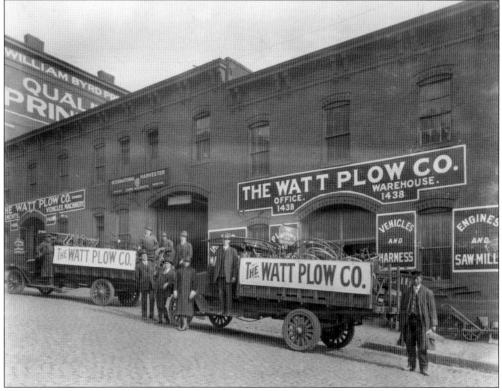

The Watt Plow Company, at Fifteenth and Franklin Streets, manufactured and sold all types of agricultural tools and implements. The city of Richmond originally consisted of farmland; it grew over the years from east to west, slowly expanding the city limits. Cotton, tobacco, and flour were major products of the region, and, prior to the Civil War, Richmond was an active slave-trading center in the South. (Courtesy of the Valentine Richmond History Center.)

In *Houses of Old Richmond*, Mary Wingfield Scott details the history of the Cole Digges house: "Thomas Rutherfoord bought a hundred-acre farm to the west of Richmond from Alexander Buchanan in 1794 and it is said that the only building on it was an overseer's house made of wood. Rutherfoord built his own home at what is now the northeast corner of Adams and Franklin streets and sold off lots to his friends in order that he might be surrounded by pleasant neighbors. Of the many houses built in what was called 'Rutherfoord's Addition', only one survives in anything like its original condition. This is the house which was apparently built in 1809 by Revolutionary War hero Cole Diggs." The Federal-style house, located at 204 West Franklin Street, today is the statewide headquarters of Preservation Virginia. (Courtesy of the Valentine Richmond History Center.)

In the early 1900s, large department stores, like Globe Clothing (right), began to proliferate on Broad Street, the main shopping district in the city for many decades. Just as the socially prominent Confederate women had led the campaign for national Confederate cemeteries and memorial celebrations, in the 1920s and 1930s, Richmond ladies Mary Wingfield Scott, Elisabeth Scott Bocock, Louise Catterall, and Mary Reed were, in large part, responsible for creating the concept of preservation in Richmond. (Both, courtesy of the Valentine Richmond History Center.)

Broad Street has always been the main commercial boulevard in Richmond, and it is lined with a wide variety of commercial buildings in architectural styles that range from Art Deco to Italianate. A trolley line running down the center of the street eventually replaced horse-and-buggy traffic in the early 20th century. (Both, courtesy of the Valentine Richmond History Center.)

A shipment of TEN SOLID CAR LOADS (400 kegs each) of the Celebrated PIEDMONT HORSE AND MULE SHOES, of the very first quality, made to one customer. This is said to be the largest single shipment of horse shoes by all rail ever made to a jobber.

THE TREDEGAR COMPANY, Richmond, Virginia

Manufacturers of Piedmont Horse and Mule Shoes.

The old advertisement pictured here highlights the railroad's prominence in the growth of the city. Richmond's railway and canal systems played a large part in its leading role as a center of commerce both prior to the Civil War and in the years that followed. George Washington helped design Richmond's canal system and served as the honorary president of the James River Company. The Kanahwa Canal was originally constructed to bypass the James River rapids that run through the city, and in 1835, the Kanawha Canal Company formed, with a plan to connect the James River to the Ohio and Mississippi Rivers. The river was used to power gristmills, helping Richmond become one of largest flour producers in America. (Courtesy of the Valentine Richmond History Center.)

Richmond was famous for its ironwork before the Civil War. This photograph shows the details on the ornate fencing and balustrade at the Bolling Haxall house, now home to the Woman's Club. (Courtesy of the Valentine Richmond History Center.)

This photograph, taken at the Bolling Haxall house at 12 East Franklin Street, highlights the cast-iron gates that graced most homes along Franklin Street in the 1800s. Many of the original gates, including those at the Linden Row Inn, still remain today. (Courtesy of the Valentine Richmond History Center.)

This view of Linden Row looking west shows many of the old linden trees for which it was originally named. Once, each yard had its own linden tree, and the porticos dripped with wisteria. The development of Franklin Street in the 19th century unfortunately destroyed many of the beautiful trees that had been a major characteristic of the residential neighborhood and that had formed a shady arcade past the stately homes. (Courtesy of the Valentine Richmond History Center.)

In her book *Houses of Old Richmond*, Mary Wingfield Scott describes brick double houses as "two-an-a-half stories with a peaked roof and a chimney made to serve both parts of the building." Pictured here, the Crump double house is a classic example of this architectural style, popular with those of modest means. (Courtesy of the Valentine Richmond History Center.)

In the 1830s, wooden cottages proliferated in various neighborhoods of Richmond. These structures, along with brick double houses, were homes for the middle class. Pictured here, the Morris Cottage at 2500 East Grace Street in Church Hill was one of three Federal-style cottages built by carpenter John Morris, who lived in the one at 207 North Twenty-fifth Street. In the Jackson Ward Historic District, the Tucker Cottage, a Colonial-style building, is one of the few remaining examples of a gambrel-roofed cottage in the city. (Courtesy of the Valentine Richmond History Center.)

Named after the famous ironworks in Tredegar, Wales, Richmond's Tredegar Iron Works produced more than 1,000 cannons for the Confederate army during the Civil War. In World War I, Tredegar once more became a center for the manufacturing of ordnance (below). It continued to operate until 1952. In 2000, the National Park Service designated Tredegar its primary visitor center for Richmond-area Civil War battlefields. (Both, courtesy of the Valentine Richmond History Center.)

Mary Wingfield Scott described the transition of Franklin Street from a residential neighborhood to a commercial zone: "The passing of Franklin Street as a street of homes began in 1927 when the Cunningham-Archer house was pulled down, to be followed two years later by the beautiful block west of it. The change from a residence to a business street was not completed when the great depression and then the second World War froze Franklin into that hopeless limbo between residences and stores which might be called the Parking Lot Period of development." (Both, courtesy of the Valentine Richmond History Center.)

This photograph shows the kind of parade Mary Wingfield Scott described passing in front of Linden Row in the early 20th century: "We could stand on the hospitable porches of friends and relatives, and shout and sing 'Dixie' as the white plumes of the Blues or the bearskin shakos of the Howitzers or the faded uniforms of the men in gray—some of them could still march in 1907—went up the street. Those who have not seen the houses draped in Confederate flags for Memorial Day or General Lee's birthday will never know what Franklin Street was. . . . Now even the blocks where an old house or two remain are pock-marked with parking lots; a great gasoline sign broods over the door through which Lee passed when he returned from Appomattox." (Courtesy of the Valentine Richmond History Center.)

In 1922, the two easternmost houses at Linden Row, 116 and 118, were demolished to make way for the Medical Arts building, pictured in the far left behind tree. As the century rolled on, the old families of Linden Row moved out, and shopkeepers moved in. Some of the houses were turned into apartments or boardinghouses. Herbert R. Perkinson remembers visiting Linden Row in his youth. "I was about 13 at the time and counted among my pasttimes walking the few blocks from the apartment over to the stamp shop run by Mr. John Dennis in the basement of a Linden Row house near the Second Street end," he recounted. "In the summertime, the basement was always a cool retreat from the city heat." (Courtesy of the Valentine Richmond History Center.)

Located at 401 West Franklin Street, the Commonwealth Club has been a private men's club for more than 100 years. Designed by New York firm Carrére and Hastings, which designed the Jefferson Hotel, the Commonwealth Club was founded in 1890 and exudes a masculine ambience. The Colonial Revival structure, featuring brick and terra-cotta, gives a nod to the Romanesque style as well. It is still one of Richmond's most exclusive private institutions, and membership is by invitation only. (Courtesy of Historic Richmond.)

By the time this photograph was taken, the residents of Linden Row had traded their stylish carriages for automobiles. The genteel life of servants preparing elaborate meals in the outdoor kitchens became a memory. In an article in the *Richmond Times*, former resident Helena Lefroy Caperton recalls, "Our early morning quiet was broken only by the swish of brooms and hose, as maids and butlers swept off and watered the fronts. Later came the clop-clop of buggies and carriages being brought around from the livery stable and hitched to the haughty iron horseheads. And then one detected the reassuring aromas of bread baking and coffee beans being roasted as cooks began preparations for breakfast in the outdoor kitchens." (Courtesy of the Library of Congress Archives.)

Irene Langhorne and her sister Nancy both attended Virginia Ellet's school for girls at Linden Row. Irene, known as a great Southern beauty who was reported to have received more than 62 marriage proposals, married artist Charles Dana Gibson. Gibson drew cartoons of early-1900s life and was known for his drawings of beautiful women. Irene is credited with being his inspiration for these portraits and is known as "the Gibson Girl." (Courtesy of the Library of Congress Archives.)

Nancy Langhorne attended Miss Jennie's School in 1895. She is reported to have had a vivacious personality and sharp wit. Her first marriage to Robert Gould Shaw was short-lived; after their divorce, she married Lord Waldorf Astor and moved to England, where she eventually became the first woman elected to the British House of Commons. This photograph was taken on January 27, 1938, when Lady Astor visited the US Senate. Pictured here are, from left to right, Sen. Joseph O'Mahoney, Sen. Hattie Caraway, Lady Astor, Sen. Harry Byrd, Sen. Key Pittman, and Sen. Claude A. Pepper. (Courtesy Library of Congress Archives.)

Irene and Nancy remained close over the years. This 1956 photograph shows the sisters, Irene (Mrs. Charles Dana Gibson) on the left, and Nancy (Viscountess Astor) at center. Also seen here are Waldorf Astor, 2nd Viscount Astor; and Nancy's son, William Waldorf Astor, 3rd Viscount Astor. (Courtesy of the Library of Congress Archives.)

Linden Row most likely looked like this when Irene and Nancy Langhorne attended Virginia Ellet's school for girls at 112 East Franklin Street and when author Mary Johnston resided at 110 East Franklin Street. While many prominent Virginia women attended Miss Jennie's School at Linden Row, Irene and Nancy are two who attained international fame in later years. (Courtesy of Valentine Richmond History Center.)

By the time Mary Johnston moved into 110 East Franklin Street with two of her sisters, she was already famous for her second novel, *To Have and to Hold*. She lived at Linden Row for six years and was part of the genteel society of the day, attending the Woman's Club, hosting teas, and playing bridge. In 1908, her novel *Lewis Rand*, set in early Richmond, was published. A proponent of women's suffrage, she continued to write and speak for that cause after she moved to Warm Springs in 1912. (Both, courtesy of the Library of Congress Archives.)

Architectural historian and Richmond preservationist Mary Wingfield Scott also attended Miss Jennie's School at Linden Row. Born into a wealthy and prominent Richmond family, Scott traveled through Europe during her youth, studied at Bryn Mawr and Barnard, and received her PhD at the University of Chicago, a rare accomplishment for a woman in the early 20th century. Her two books, *Houses of Old Richmond* and *Old Richmond Neighborhoods*, are still considered to be definitive and well-researched resources on Richmond's architectural history. (Courtesy of Alfred Scott.)

By the late 1940s, Broad Street had become a modern thoroughfare, and the trolley cars were a thing of the past. Broad Street was still the major shopping district in Richmond, but many of the old buildings were replaced with modern retailers, like the Miller & Rhoads Department Store (below). It became an iconic part of Richmond, and shoppers would travel from surrounding cities, like Williamsburg and Fredericksburg, especially during the holidays. Today, the building has been transformed into a Hilton Garden Inn, but the exterior sign and a photograph gallery of the store's 105-year history pay homage to the role that Miller & Rhoads played in the city. (Both, courtesy of Historic Richmond.)

In her book *Houses of Old Richmond*, Mary Wingfield Scott wrote, "From the earliest times Richmond had been a centre of trade, based on the system of commission merchants who exchanged the raw-materials of a new country for the manufactured products of an old one." By the 1950s and 1960s, Richmond was still a center of trade, but no longer a manufacturing or agricultural center. While it still included some large tobacco companies, Richmond had become more of a banking and financial center. Pictured on the right is the Art Deco Central National Bank building, erected in 1929. The ornate Loew's Movie Palace (below) opened in 1928 and is now part of the city's performing-arts complex, Richmond Center Stage. (Both, Courtesy of Historic Richmond.)

This 1957 photograph shows Linden Row as it looked when Mary Wingfield Scott purchased the seven buildings numbered 100–112. The house at 114 East Franklin Street still stands, but it has been privately owned for many years. The easternmost houses, at 116 and 118, were torn down and replaced by the Medical Arts building, which eventually became Linden Towers Apartments. When asked why she purchased Linden Row, Scott told Anne Hobson Freeman in an interview, "I was down at St. Paul's at early church one morning and the Lord said to me just as plain as anything in the world, 'Buy it if you have to go to the poorhouse.'" (Courtesy of the Valentine Richmond History Center.)

Four

Mary Wingfield Scott Saves Linden Row

"How can you call Franklin Street an old neighborhood now? Ask those who remember when the social ambition of every Richmonder was to live on Franklin Street. Those of us who never attained this ideal of elegance could at least take part in the Easter parade . . . or stand on the hospitable porches of friends and shout and sing 'Dixie' as the white plumes of the Blues or the bearskin shakos of the Howitzers or the faded uniforms of the men in gray went up the street. Those who have not seen the houses draped in Confederate flags for Memorial Day or General Lee's birthday will never know what Franklin Street was.

There are still the verandas on the James Anderson and Lyons houses, the balcony and casting on the Frank Williams house, and the fence of the Woman's Club to recall all the beautiful ironwork that is gone. Above all, Linden Row is still there. 'When Linden Row is gone, I'll never drive down Franklin again,' says one Richmond woman, not old enough to remember the street in its heyday, yet with the taste and perception to realize that Linden Row sums up and symbolizes the dignity and grace of Richmond's architecture and life.

The change from a residence to a business street was not completed when the Great Depression and then World War II froze Franklin Street into that hopeless limbo between residences and stores—what might be called the Parking Lot Period of development.

If the owners of fine old houses can no longer live in them, and yet have a pride in their preservation, let them turn these mansions into apartments, always in demand downtown, or let them stretch every effort to make it possible for organizations to buy them. Then future visitors to Richmond will carry away memories of Franklin Street different from, but just as ineradicable, as the memories of those who enjoyed its hospitality 30 years ago."

Mary Wingfield Scott, author
"Old Neighborhoods of Richmond: Franklin Retains Vestiges of Past"
Richmond Daily Dispatch, October 25, 1942

Born in 1895 to a wealthy Richmond family, Mary "Winkie" Wingfield Scott grew up in a privileged environment in the Franklin Street neighborhood, at the time one of the most desirable addresses in the city. She attended the finest private schools, including Virginia Ellet's school for girls at Linden Row, pictured here, and often traveled with her family in Europe. "We had poetry to learn at Miss Jennie's, chiefly from Lily West, whom I didn't like anyway, so maybe that was why I didn't cotton up to poetry. But I did like history, and especially anything connected with English history," Wingfield recalled. "Our homeroom teacher at Miss Jennie's was Miss Lulie Blair, who was an actress manqué: she never wore corsets, as they were called in that day." Ironically, Mary Wingfield Scott ended up owning the Linden Row house in which she had attended Miss Jennie's School. (Courtesy of Alfred Scott.)

In the introduction to *Winkie*, a collection of Mary Wingfield Scott's own memoirs, published interviews, and the recollections of friends, Alfred Scott writes, "The era of Progress and More Smokestacks, in the 1920's, accomplished for the residential part of old Richmond what the Evacuation Fire of 1865 had for the business district. After studying at Bryn Mawr and Barnard, and receiving her Ph.D. at the University of Chicago, she returned to Richmond and with increasing indignation watched the old houses of her childhood disappearing one by one. Gradually she made saving them an avocation." The Kent-Valentine House is seen here with its original iron verandah, although the ornate ironwork was replaced with a portico in later years. As a child, "Winkie," as her family called her, would have known the house as it is seen here. (Courtesy of Alfred Scott.)

This photograph of the Fred Scott family was taken at 909 West Franklin Street in the formal parlor as a memento for Buford, who was going off to war. Mary Wingfield Scott's grandfather, Maj. Frederic R. Scott, moved to Richmond in 1872. In 1881, he began building a home at 712 West Franklin Street, which became the Scott family gathering place or, as Winkie called it, "the family home, headquarters, castle." From 1883 to 1937, when her infamous Aunt Boxie died, 712 West Franklin Street played a central role in Winkie's life. (Courtesy of Alfred Scott.)

The Scott family often got together for holiday dinners, hunt breakfasts, and regular visits in one of their homes in the Franklin Street neighborhood. This undated photograph is from Mary Wingfield Scott's personal photo album. The persons identified on the back of the photograph are, in no particular order, Frederick Campbell, Uncle George, Aunt Boxie, Aunt Dora (wife of Uncle Tom), Aunt Mary Hamilton, Aunt Elise (Mrs. Fred Scott), Mrs. Strother (Coz. Emily, Mrs. Nelson Strother), Mrs. Christine Bell, Mr. (Nelson) Strother, and Uncle Tom. (Courtesy of Alfred Scott.)

"I lived just around the corner [from the Frederic Scott family home]," Mary Wingfield Scott recalled in her unpublished autobiography. "What did we do at 712 that it should have been such a paradise to us children? Day in and day out, we played paper dolls on the marble base of the tall pier-glass. Our chief entertainment, it is sad to report, was Theft. Almonds, stuffed dates from the china cupboard, thin-biscuit from the pantry, sugar lumps from the big silver sugar dish all vanished into a cache kept under the chiffonier in Mama Scott's room." (Courtesy of Alfred Scott.)

Mary Wingfield Scott received a PhD in art and art history from the University of Chicago during an era when few women went to college. She published two books on the architecture and history of Richmond, *Houses of Old Richmond* in 1941 and *Old Richmond Neighborhoods* in 1950. Both books are considered definitive texts on the city's surviving and demolished historic structures. She was instrumental in the foundation of the William Byrd Branch of the Association for the Preservation of Virginia Antiquities (APVA), whose members are pictured here, when the Craig House was threatened with demolition in 1935. (Courtesy of the Valentine Richmond History Center.)

In her book *Houses of Old Richmond*, Mary Wingfield Scott details the history of the Adam Craig House, built sometime between 1784 and 1787: "Our first knowledge of what the buildings included comes from Craig's insuring all his property in 1796. On the four lots were, first, a one-story 'Dutch roof' cottage, the 'Office of County Court,' at the northeast corner of Eighteenth and Grace. East of that was the present house, which on the plat looks just as it does today, with its ell, two stories, and three porches. Behind it was a one-story wooden kitchen, replaced before 1815 by the present brick kitchen, which doubtless utilized from the earlier building the chimney with its big fireplaces and iron cranes. East of these, facing Nineteenth Street, was a one-story wooden house, used as a lodging house, with a wooden kitchen back of it, on Nineteenth also." (Both, courtesy of the Valentine Richmond History Center.)

The threatened destruction of the Adam Craig House was the impetus for the formation of the William Byrd Branch of the APVA. Mary Wingfield Scott's partner, Virginia Withers, wrote of that event: "It was 1935. Fortunately, it was Mary who was late for lunch without telephoning that it would be unnecessary to arrange for a funeral. A champion worrier herself, she'd have taken it hard if any other member of the family had pulled such a stunt on her. But she didn't stop to apologize when she burst in, her face lit up like a constellation. 'Don't faint. I've bought a house,' she announced." (Both, courtesy of the Valentine Richmond History Center.)

Mary Wingfield Scott and Elizabeth Bocock led the movement to start the William Byrd Branch of the APVA specifically to save the Craig House. Alfred Scott remembers the two ladies, noting, "I'm reminded that Mary Wingfield Scott and Elizabeth Bocock were both of the 'never ask permission' frame of mind, and when they got their minds on something, woe betide anyone who got in their way." Scott educated the public on the value of architectural preservation through her newsletter *Old Richmond News* by leading tours through historic neighborhoods (below), and in her two books on Richmond's architectural history, *Houses of Old Richmond* and *Old Richmond Neighborhoods*. Her books are still the bibles of Richmond architectural history and are available digitally with free downloads from the websites of the Valentine Richmond History Center, Preservation Virginia, Historic Richmond, and www.rosegill.com. (Both, courtesy of the Valentine Richmond History Center.)

The Greek Revival structure known as the Allen Double House, built in 1836, is just one block south of the Linden Row Inn, at 4 and 6 East Main Street. It is one of the earliest buildings in the district known as Monroe Ward. Historic Richmond renovated the houses in 2000 and located its headquarters at 4 East Main Street. (Courtesy of Historic Richmond.)

By 1949, the remaining houses of Linden Row were in severe danger of being bulldozed. The Richmond Planning Commission approved a plan to rezone the entire block from residential to commercial, which would have been the death knell for the Greek Revival row. In 1950, Mary Wingfield Scott purchased the westernmost houses of 100, 102, and 104 East Franklin Street, and a few years later, obtained 106, 108, 110, and 112. For more than 20 years, she served as a landlord while maintaining and preserving the original architectural features of Linden Row on both the interior and exterior of the houses. The house at 114 has remained under private ownership to this day. (Courtesy of the Valentine Richmond History Center.)

Mary Wingfield Scott, pictured in the Valentine garden, lived from 1923 until 1967 with Virginia Withers, a relationship that she describes as "rocky." In 1927, she and "Ginnie" adopted two boys, something as unheard of at that time, as was their same-sex relationship. Both of the women had a grandmother named Walker, and thus, the boys became Robert "Bobby" Edward Walker and John "Johnny" Patrick Walker. In 1929, they took Bobby and Johnny to France and spent two years there, eventually returning to Richmond. Scott recounted, "Our relationship was stabilized by having taken on the two boys, and we felt it would be an unpardonable thing to interfere with their home life." Scott helped Withers start the Top Knot Nursery School, writing, "She proved a genius, and really found herself dealing with little children." And while Ginnie was described as gentle and creative, Winkie's family, friends, and preservation colleagues described "Mary Wing" as "outspoken," somewhat of a euphemism for her gruff demeanor and lack of personal warmth. (Courtesy of the Valentine Richmond History Center.)

In an interview with Anne Hobson Freeman, Mary Wingfield Scott described the state of Linden Row when she purchased the houses. "You wouldn't believe the condition of some of those houses when I got them. The corner house had been a rooming house and was filled with filthy old mattresses and dead rats. I remember an old wooden pail with salt herring in it sitting in the middle of the former parlor. Believe me, I didn't eat them." In her book *Old Richmond Neighborhoods*, Scott writes of Linden Row, "What these houses lacked in variety and originality, they compensated for in dignity and harmony." To Scott, the simple brick facades and graceful Greek Revival porticos "gave more of the atmosphere of Franklin Street as it used to be than any other building not to mention block still standing." (Courtesy of Historic Richmond.)

While the Linden Row houses were simple and elegant, Mary Wingfield Scott felt details like the period windows and cast-iron fencing and gates were important to preserve. She cleaned up the property, collected period chandeliers, pier mirrors, and mantel mirrors, and even laid brick herself in the courtyard, while preserving the interior architectural details, including ceiling medallions, cornices, marble mantels, and original woodwork. She would not even allow her tenants to install window air-conditioning units, since they did not fit with the period she was preserving. (Both, courtesy of Historic Richmond.)

Mary Wingfield Scott may have been a member of one of Richmond's leading families, but she was known as an outspoken and eccentric woman. She was often seen in her fur coat, high-top tennis shoes, and dress, digging in the garden, laying bricks, or climbing trees to take photographs of houses that interested her. She used her newsletter to the members of the William Byrd Branch of the APVA to take the city and other property owners to task over preservation issues, saying once, "There will always be people with no taste and they will be in the majority." (Courtesy of the *Richmond Times-Dispatch*.)

During her tenure as a landlord at Linden Row, Mary Wingfield Scott's friends pitched in to help her restore the grounds, and she created a plaque that read "in grateful recognition of those firms and individuals whose co-operation has made the restoration of Linden Row a joyous adventure." For 35 years, Susie Henley (seen below) cared for the inside of the houses, and for more than two decades, Joe Monroe (above) cared for the grounds, working side-by-side with Scott (also pictured) more often than not. (Both, courtesy of Alfred Scott.)

Mary Wingfield Scott, pictured center with her back toward the camera, continued her efforts to educated Richmond residents and what she called "the bulldozing brigade" of city officials and developers as to the value of preserving the city's unique architectural history. In 1980, she donated Linden Row to the Historic Richmond Foundation (now called Historic Richmond) with the proviso that the organization retain control of the design and first right of refusal on the property in perpetuity should it sell it to a private buyer. (Courtesy of the Valentine Richmond History Center.)

When Mary Wingfield Scott died in 1983, the *Richmond Times-Dispatch* wrote, "Miss Scott was known for her effectiveness, her hard work, her scholarly background, but not for her tact." In May 1992, Scott's family and more than 200 well-wishers and Richmond city officials gathered in her memory in the alley behind Linden Row Inn to install a European-style street sign designating it "Miss Scott's Alley." Scott's niece and namesake, seen here at right, wore high-top tennis shoes in her honor. (Courtesy of the *Richmond Times-Dispatch*.)

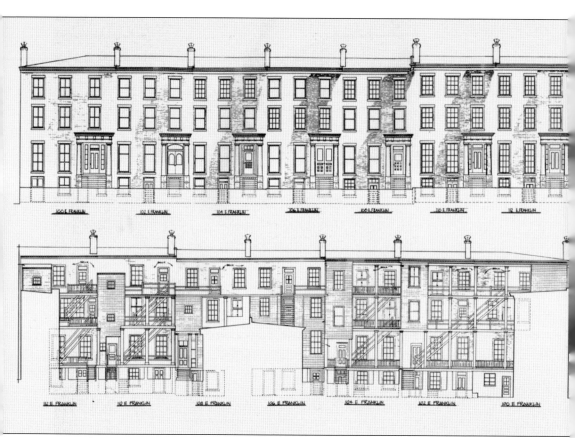

In 1985, Historic Richmond accepted a proposal from Southeastern Historic Properties, Inc. to purchase Linden Row and convert it into a small inn. The proposal was accepted because the company's plan was to preserve both the exterior structure and the interior architectural details of Linden Row, keeping the historic integrity of the houses intact. The initial architectural drawing shows the plan for the exterior of the new inn. (Courtesy of Historic Richmond.)

The most significant renovation to Linden Row was the rebuilding of the three-story rear porch, which had rotted in many places. An additional six feet was added to its depth, to accommodate the addition of modern bathrooms for the rear rooms and to structure the porch to become the main corridor for access to the rooms. Of the seven houses, six retained their four-floor stair halls. (Both, courtesy of Alfred Scott.)

On the Franklin Street facade of Linden Row, many of the windows were restored to their original small-pane configuration. In the rear garden and courtyard, brick paving was restored, and the grounds were planted with many of the same varieties of trees, shrubs, perennials, and bulbs that had grown there in past centuries. The garden restoration and new fountain were made possible by special funds donated by Sally Dickenson Todd in memory of Mary Wingfield Scott and Scott's lifelong friends Virginia Withers and Rachael Wilson. (Both, courtesy of Alfred Scott.)

On September 23, 1988, Historic Richmond held a grand ball on First Street in front of the entrance to the new Linden Row Inn, and on October 26, the inn welcomed its first guests. To complete the old-world ambience of the inn, the wonderful collection of gasoliers, pier mirrors, and mantel mirrors that Mary Wingfield Scott had collected were loaned to the inn, while remaining under Historic Richmond's ownership. (Photograph by Richard Creek, courtesy of Historic Richmond.)

Managed by Great Inns of America, the inn welcomed its first guests in October 1988 and held a grand opening the following January. The rooms contained a mix of antiques on loan from the Historic Richmond Foundation and period reproductions. (Both, courtesy of Historic Richmond.)

The Dining Room and the courtyard fountain of Linden Row Inn, seen here in the late 1980s and the 1990s, look much the same today. The reproduction iron fountain, with its refurbished herringbone brick pattern, is a focal point in the courtyard. (Both, courtesy of Linden Row Inn.)

At the time of the renovation and opening of the first incarnation of the inn, there were no such things as flat-screen televisions or wireless Internet. Current owners of the Linden Row Inn, Savara Properties Inc., have updated the linens and the furnishings, as well as the high-tech amenities, in the Parlour Suites and throughout the inn's rooms. However, it is important to note that the original woodwork, chandeliers, and period details have not changed with ownership of the property. (Both, courtesy of Linden Row Inn.)

While the courtyard looks much the same more than 25 years after its restoration, the Garden Rooms in the brick dependencies have changed significantly. (Both, courtesy of Linden Row Inn.)

While the Victorian floral carpets and furniture are typical of the earlier era and a good representation of that period at Linden Row, Savara Properties Inc. has updated the Parlour Suites with a mix of antiques and traditional 21st-century furnishings. (Both, courtesy of Linden Row Inn.)

Five

THE LINDEN ROW
INN TODAY

Owning and operating a hotel within a treasured historic building certainly has its challenges. However, the Linden Row Inn is the jewel in the company's portfolio of assets, and the Savara team has made a strong commitment to preserving the historical integrity of the property while ensuring that its services and amenities meet the needs of modern travelers.

Linden Row Inn today is still a vibrant part of Richmond's downtown, delighting visitors with its old-world charm and with modern amenities. Featuring 70 elegant guestrooms, including seven spacious suites, with spa-style granite bathrooms, complimentary wireless Internet service, flat-screen televisions, coffeemakers, hairdryers, and upscale bath amenities, the rooms are located in the seven four-story row houses and in the two carriage houses in the secluded garden.

Other amenities include complimentary shuttle service within a two-mile radius, access to the nearby state-of-the-art YMCA fitness center, premium wine and beer service, and valet parking. Both the Dining Room and Board Room are popular for meetings and special events, and the Garden Courtyard, with its brick patio, tree-lined walls, and sparkling fountain, is one of Richmond's most popular venues for spring and summer weddings.

And just as it is the residents who make a house a home, it is the genuinely friendly and attentive service of the Linden Row Inn staff that makes this boutique hotel feel like a home away from home for regular guests who return year after year.

Savara Properties Inc. believes that it is a privilege to own a treasured asset like the Linden Row Inn and looks forward to ensuring that future generations are able to walk in the footsteps of history at this unique hotel.

Acquired by Savara Properties Inc. in 2008, this 70-room boutique hotel is within walking distance of several downtown historic attractions and offers free shuttle service within a two-mile radius. The exterior doors to the gracious row homes are now locked for security, although the lovely columns and intricate iron gates have remained the same. Parlour Suites are located on the main level, or second floor, while Main House rooms are located on the first, third, and fourth floors, where the homes' original bedrooms were once located. Both can be accessed by either an elevator or stairway. (Courtesy of Linden Row Inn.)

Linden Row Inn is located at the corner of First and Franklin Streets, with its entrance on First Street. A charming sign on the corner directs guests to the entrance. First Street is a one-way street heading south toward the James River, and Franklin Street is one-way heading east, so it is necessary to access First Street from either Grace Street or Broad Street to the north. (Courtesy of Linden Row Inn.)

The inn's valet is happy to retrieve guest cars upon request during operating hours, and there is no limit on the number of times one may take their car in and out of the garage. (Courtesy of Linden Row Inn.)

Grace Street is one block north of the inn, and Main Street is one block south. Broad Street, two blocks to the north, is a dining and entertainment corridor with several fine restaurants and the popular music venue the National Theatre. Virginia Commonwealth University's basketball arena, the Siegel Center, is also located on Broad Street. The hotel is also located within walking distance of the Greater Richmond Convention Center. Architectural historian Robert P. Winthrop called the row "the finest terrace row of pre–Civil War houses in the city and perhaps in the South." (Courtesy of Linden Row Inn.)

Guests of the Linden Row Inn also have access to the downtown YMCA, located just one block west on Franklin Street, just past the corner of North Foushee Street. Two blocks south of the hotel, Cary Street to the east is a popular restaurant and shopping district that slopes down to Shockoe Bottom, where visitors can access the mile-long Canal Walk. (Courtesy of Linden Row Inn.)

Throughout the Linden Row Inn, antiques on loan from Historic Richmond are featured in public spaces, like the comfortable Parlour Lobby, as well as in many Main House rooms and Parlour Suites. The lobby offers a complimentary computer station for guest use, as well as comfortable sofas and chairs for reading or relaxing. Several albums with historic photographs of Linden Row and other memorabilia are displayed in the lobby area, which also displays contemporary artwork from 1708 Gallery, a local nonprofit gallery. (Courtesy of Linden Row Inn.)

The courtyard patio area just off the lobby and directly across from the Dining Room offers tables with umbrellas for alfresco dining. In addition to the complimentary coffee and tea available 24 hours a day, the inn also sells a selection or premium beer and wine á la carte. (Courtesy of Linden Row Inn.)

The seven spacious Parlour Suites are each furnished with one-of-a-kind antiques on loan from Historic Richmond that are either original to the property or the period. Each suite has 12-foot ceilings, original light fixtures, marble fireplaces, and floor-to-ceiling windows, and each suite is named after a person with historical ties to the property. Room 208 (pictured) is named after Mary Wingfield Scott, the Richmond architectural historian and preservationist who saved Linden Row from destruction. In 2009, the Savara team completely restored the Mary Wingfield Scott suite, a process that was featured on the TLC channel. She purchased seven of the eight surviving houses in the 1950s and operated them as apartments. She preserved the elaborate fireplace mantels, pier mirrors, chandeliers, original woodwork, and other period details. Before her death, she donated the houses to the Historic Richmond Foundation (now known as Historic Richmond). (Courtesy of Linden Row Inn.)

Parlour Suite 216 is named after Charles Ellis, the wealthy merchant who owned the site now occupied by the Linden Row Inn. Ellis, who lived across the street, used the property as a private garden, and it was here that his children played with Edgar Allan Poe. Poe's adopted father, John Allan, was the business partner of Charles Ellis, and the Allan family lived for a time in the Ellis house. Originally, the bedrooms of each Linden Row house were located on the upper floors. At that time, the second floor, opening off the foyer at the main front door, contained double parlors separated by pocket doors. The front parlor was for receiving company, while the back parlor was a library-like lounging area for the family. (Both, courtesy of Linden Row Inn.)

The addition of Wi-Fi service, flat-screen televisions, and modern granite bathrooms blend seamlessly with the period antiques and furnishings in the inn's seven Parlour Suites and Main House rooms. Original features, including the ornate fireplace mantels and pier mirrors, bring the past to life. Other modern amenities, including refrigerators and microwaves, are tucked into reproduction armoires. Many of the Main House's king and double rooms also contain antiques on loan from Historic Richmond, as well as fireplace mantels and period woodwork. (Both, courtesy of Linden Row Inn.)

The inn offers a complimentary continental breakfast that includes a wide selection of pastries, breads, fresh fruit, cereal, yogurt, and juices, along with hot oatmeal and waffles. The charming breakfast room was once part of the 19th-century horse stables. As late as the early 20th century, the kitchens of the Linden Row houses were located in the dependencies behind the homes. Helena Lefroy Caperton, who was born and raised at Linden Row, says, "The Linden Row houses were all alike, three stories and a basement with brick kitchens and 'offices' in the backyards. Our dining rooms were in the front room of the basement. The food was all cooked in the outdoor kitchens, both in the winter and in summer, and brought to our house across the backyard, down the area steps, through the pantry, and into the dining room." (Both, courtesy of Linden Row Inn.)

The brick courtyard (above) looks much the same as it has for more than a century, and it contains many of the same varieties of plants, trees, and shrubs. When the Linden Row houses were converted to an inn, the brick paving in the rear garden was restored, a fountain was added, and the grounds were replanted. The most significant alteration to the original structures was the rebuilding of the three-story deck (below), made deeper to accommodate the addition of bathrooms on the rear rooms on each level. Historic Richmond supervised the renovation and worked closely with the Richmond architectural firm Glave Newman Anderson on both the exterior and interior designs. (Both, courtesy of Linden Row Inn.)

Intimate and cozy, the Garden Rooms are located in the two brick dependencies in the courtyard. Built in the late 1800s, these buildings once housed kitchens, service areas, and servants' rooms. Today, they are furnished with whitewashed furniture and decorated in a floral motif. Most Garden Rooms offer direct access to the landscaped courtyard. While smaller in size, the Garden Rooms include the same modern amenities that the Main House rooms have, including flat-screen televisions and complimentary Wi-Fi. Some Garden Rooms include desks. (Both, courtesy of Linden Row Inn.)

While the Main House rooms have high ceilings and period details, including original fireplaces and mantels, the decor is more contemporary than that of the Parlour Suites. Some of the Main House rooms do contain period antiques that blend well with the traditional styling and modern amenities. While all rooms have the same modern amenities, not all rooms have desks, refrigerators, or microwaves, so guests with specific needs should request those amenities when reserving. (Both, courtesy of Linden Row Inn.)

All of the Main House rooms have direct access to the veranda, and many feature large windows, combined with high ceilings, giving them a light and spacious feel. When the Linden Row houses were private residences, bedrooms were located on the upper floors, as are Main House rooms today. In fact, the restoration was so meticulous that each townhouse could be restored to a private residence in the future. (Courtesy of Linden Row Inn.)

When Linden Row was converted to an inn, the courtyard was renovated, and a lovely fountain was added directly off the Board Room event space and visible through its French doors. (Courtesy of Linden Row Inn.)

The historic courtyard at the Linden Row Inn, where Edgar Allan Poe first courted Elmira Royster, is a wonderful setting for an outdoor wedding. Wedding season runs from April through October, and with the combined outdoor and indoor event space, the inn can accommodate up to 90 guests for a seated meal, 125 guests seated theater-style, and up to 100 guests for a buffet-style reception. (Courtesy of Linden Row Inn.)

The Linden Row Inn has a preferred list of caterers for weddings and social events. There are several setup options, from food stations and buffets to seated dinners, using indoor event space, the courtyard, or a combination of the two. (Both, courtesy of Linden Row Inn.)

Over the years, the Linden Row Inn has hosted many weddings with period themes, from Victorian vintage weddings to Civil War–era ceremonies. Parlour Suites offer a perfect backdrop for wedding photographs. (Courtesy of Linden Row Inn.)

In 1847, Fleming James built the first houses of Linden Row, across from what was known then as Linden Square. Parlour Suite 218, named in his honor, is located in 106 East Franklin Street, once the home of Virginia Pegram and her school for girls. Former Linden Row resident Helena Lefroy Caperton described the original parlors in her 1949 article in the *Richmond Times*: "Between the windows stood a tall, narrow mirror on a gold and marble stand. Art was recognized by certain colored engravings in ornate, gilded and velvet frames . . . the floors were covered with floral velvet carpets tacked from wall to wall. This décor is being revived today in period rooms and can be lovely as it was in those parlors of long ago when illuminated by the gas chandelier with crystal globes and pendants." (Both, courtesy of Linden Row Inn.)

Linden Row Inn's Board Room opens through French doors directly onto the Garden Terrace, perfect for indoor/outdoor entertaining and for wedding receptions. Used in combination with the terrace, the Board Room can accommodate up to 130 guests. The 505-square-foot indoor space can accommodate a seated dinner for 30. (Both, courtesy of Linden Row Inn.)

The Garden Courtyard offers many options for wedding receptions, including table seating and cocktail tables. There is plenty of room for a stage area for live entertainment, and the courtyard fountain adds to the ambience. (Both, courtesy of Linden Row Inn.)

Weddings are held from April through October at the inn, and several options are available for tented spaces for the ceremony and reception. (Both, courtesy of Linden Row Inn.)

The Board Room at Linden Row Inn is often used for meetings and classes. It can be set up with audio-visual equipment or in any configuration per client request. It can accommodate 40 people theater-style and 25 with a classroom-style setup. (Both, courtesy of Linden Row Inn.)

Both the Board Room and the charming Dining Room are popular for intimate luncheons, meetings, or dinners. The Board Room can accommodate up to 30 guests for a sit-down meal, and it can be set up as a buffet area. The Dining Room, with its cozy fireplace, can accommodate up to 40 people for a seated function, 50 people theater-style, and 40 people classroom-style. (Both, courtesy of Linden Row Inn.)

After saving Linden Row in the 1950s, Mary Wingfield Scott operated the houses as apartments for more than 20 years. In 1980, she donated the houses to what was then called the Historic Richmond Foundation (now Historic Richmond). In the deed transferring ownership, Scott gave the Historic Richmond Foundation design control and a right of first refusal on the property in perpetuity. Historic Richmond is still involved with the Linden Row Inn today, working closely with Savara Properties Inc. to ensure the preservation of these historic houses. (Courtesy of Alfred Scott.)

As a Richmond resident once told Mary Wingfield Scott, "When Linden Row goes, I'll never drive down Franklin again." If not for Scott's vision and passion for preserving the past, Richmond residents and visitors alike would have lost a treasured piece of the city's history. Regarding that resident, Scott said she was "one Richmond woman, not old enough to remember the street in its heyday, yet with the taste and perception to realize that Linden Row sums up and symbolizes the dignity and grace of Richmond's architecture and life." (Courtesy of the Valentine Richmond History Center.)

Thanks to Mary Wingfield Scott, Historic Richmond, and Savara Properties Inc., the Linden Row Inn today has preserved not only an important part of Richmond's architectural history, but also a gracious style of living from an earlier era. While servants may not be preparing breakfast in the outdoor kitchens and serving them under silver Sheffield domes, the upscale amenities at the Linden Row Inn and the genuine Southern hospitality of the friendly staff offer visitors a taste of the genteel life from past centuries. (Both, courtesy of Linden Row Inn.)

Formed by Elisabeth Scott Bocock and Louise Catterall in 1956, Historic Richmond Foundation (HRF), now known as Historic Richmond, was an organization that furthered the preservation work initiated in the 1930s by the William Byrd Branch. HRF worked with state senators and local government to establish the Local Old & Historic District. Today, this is an important city ordinance that creates a layer of protection against demolition and significant alteration to structures in historic districts. Analogous to the William Byrd Branch, HRF purchased significant historic structures in jeopardy of demolition. (Photograph by Richard Creek, courtesy of Historic Richmond.)

The Virginia Landmarks Register describes Linden Row as follows: "The simple, straightforward design of the facades serves to set off the beautifully executed Greek Doric dwarf porticos sheltering the entrances." Thanks to the continuing stewardship of Savara Properties Inc. and Historic Richmond, local residents and visitors to the city will be able to enjoy the stunning architecture and history of the Linden Row Inn for many years to come. (Courtesy of Linden Row Inn.)

HISTORIC RICHMOND AND THE VALENTINE RICHMOND HISTORY CENTER

HISTORIC RICHMOND: Historic Richmond, formerly known as Historic Richmond Foundation, is an organization dedicated to preserving and protecting the foundation of what makes Richmond unique, beautiful, and unlike any other city on the planet. It is a 501(c)3 nonprofit that works to encourage preservation, rehabilitation, and revitalization in the city.

Historic Richmond collaborates with government, neighborhoods, businesses, organizations, foundations, and individuals that share its passion for Richmond's significant and historic structures and places. The organization considers it its job to educate and enlighten citizens about the cultural, aesthetic, and economic value of Richmond's unique built environment. It engages the community all year long through a regular flow of information and publications, public events, presentations, and special tours.

Historic Richmond believes this city is like no other on Earth, and it is doing everything possible to keep it that way. To learn how you can get involved, visit www.historicrichmond.com.

VALENTINE RICHMOND HISTORY CENTER: The Valentine Richmond History Center has been collecting, preserving, and interpreting Richmond's 400-year history for over a century. Located in the heart of historic downtown, the history center is a place for residents and tourists to discover the diverse stories that tell the broader history of this important region. A comprehensive program of exhibitions, tours, special events, research opportunities, school programs, and other public programs engage the broadest audience in an ongoing dialogue about the significance and relevance of the city's history. The mission of the Richmond History Center is to engage, educate, and challenge a diverse audience by collecting, preserving, and interpreting Richmond's history.

The history of the institution begins with Mann S. Valentine Jr., the museum's founder, who made his fortune with the creation and production of Valentine's Meat Juice, a health tonic made from pure beef juice. As did many men of his era, Mann Valentine collected artifacts. His collection may have begun, as rumored, with a cigar box filled with arrowheads, but it soon grew to comprise hundreds of objects. He shared his love of history with his brother, renowned sculptor Edward V. Valentine. Mann Valentine laid the foundation for the museum in 1892; when he died in 1893, he provided the original bequest for the Valentine Museum, leaving his personal collection of art and artifacts and the 1812 Wickham House.

The Valentine Museum, the first private museum in the city of Richmond, opened in 1898; Edward Valentine served as its first president, from its opening until his death in 1930. In his own will, he left an incredible collection of his sculpture, papers, furniture, and memorabilia to the museum that still bears his family name.

Over time, the institution has evolved from a general art and history museum to one focusing on the life and history of Richmond, Virginia. For more than 100 years, the Richmond History Center has collected, preserved, and interpreted the materials of Richmond's life and history. Through its collections, exhibitions, and programs, it reflects and interprets the broad issues and diverse communities that define the history of Richmond and its surrounding counties. The history center is the only institution in the city committed solely to this mission. Visit the center online at www.richmondhistorycenter.com.

DISCOVER THOUSANDS OF LOCAL HISTORY BOOKS FEATURING MILLIONS OF VINTAGE IMAGES

Arcadia Publishing, the leading local history publisher in the United States, is committed to making history accessible and meaningful through publishing books that celebrate and preserve the heritage of America's people and places.

Find more books like this at
www.arcadiapublishing.com

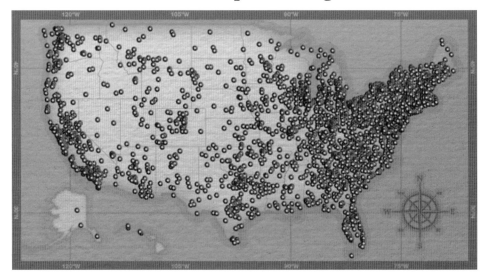

Search for your hometown history, your old stomping grounds, and even your favorite sports team.